W9-BFD-579

Betsy Ross

A Buddy Book
by
Christy DeVillier

ABDO
Publishing Company

VISIT US AT

www.abdopublishing.com

Published by ABDO Publishing Company, 8000 West 78th Street, Edina, Minnesota 55439. Copyright © 2004 by Abdo Consulting Group, Inc. International copyrights reserved in all countries. No part of this book may be reproduced in any form without written permission from the publisher.

Printed in the United States of America, North Mankato, Minnesota.
012004 032011

Edited by: Michael P. Goecke
Contributing Editor: Matt Ray
Image Research: Deborah Coldiron
Graphic Design: Jane Halbert
Cover Photograph: Library of Congress
Interior Photographs/Illustrations: Hulton Archives, Library of Congress, North Wind

Library of Congress Cataloging-in-Publication Data

DeVillier, Christy, 1971–
    Betsy Ross / Christy DeVillier.
        v. cm. — (First biographies)
    Includes index.
    Contents: Who is Betsy Ross?—Growing up—Quaker life—Learning upholstery—Meeting John Ross—American Revolution—Legend of the flag—Famous patriot.
    ISBN 1-59197-516-6
    1. Ross, Betsy, 1752–1836—Juvenile literature. 2. Revolutionaries—United States—Biography—Juvenile literature. 3. United States—History—Revolution, 1775–1783—Flags—Juvenile literature. 4. Flags—United States—History—18th century—Juvenile literature. [1. Ross, Betsy, 1752–1836. 2. Revolutionaries. 3. Flags—United States. 4. Women—Biography.] I. Title.

E302.6.R77D48 2004
973.3'092—dc21
[B]

                                                                2003052259

Table Of Contents

Who Is Betsy Ross?

Betsy Ross was an American Patriot. She lived during the Revolutionary War.

Betsy Ross was skilled at sewing. Many people believe she sewed the first Stars and Stripes flag. "Stars and Stripes" is another name for the flag of the United States.

BETSEY ROSS

Betsy Ross may have sewed
the first Stars and Stripes flag.

Growing Up

Betsy was born on January 1, 1752. Her parents named her Elizabeth. But they called her Betsy.

Betsy's parents were Samuel and Rebecca Griscom. They lived in Pennsylvania. Back then, Pennsylvania was a colony ruled by Britain.

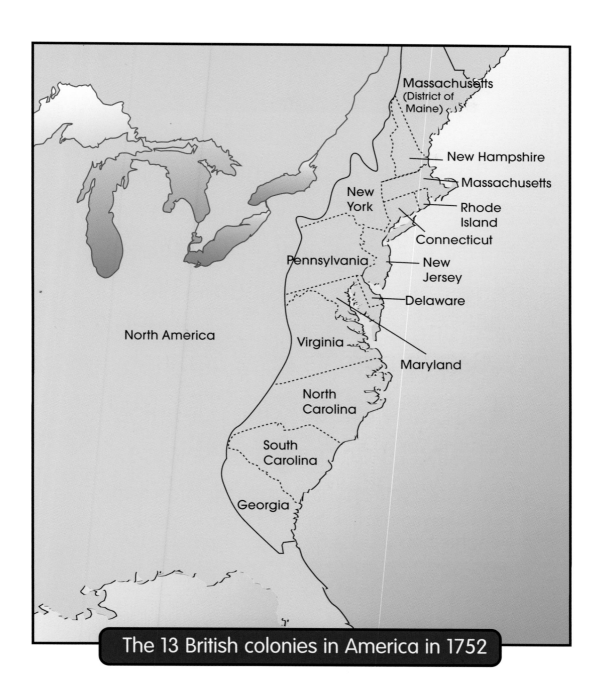

Massachusetts
(District of
Maine)

New Hampshire

Massachusetts

New
York

Rhode
Island

Connecticut

Pennsylvania

New
Jersey

Delaware

North America

Virginia

Maryland

North
Carolina

South
Carolina

Georgia

The 13 British colonies in America in 1752

Betsy grew up in Philadelphia, Pennsylvania. She went to Friends Public School. Betsy learned to read and write. She learned to add and subtract.

At home, Betsy helped her family. She did cooking, cleaning, washing, mending, and sewing. For fun, Betsy went on picnics with her family.

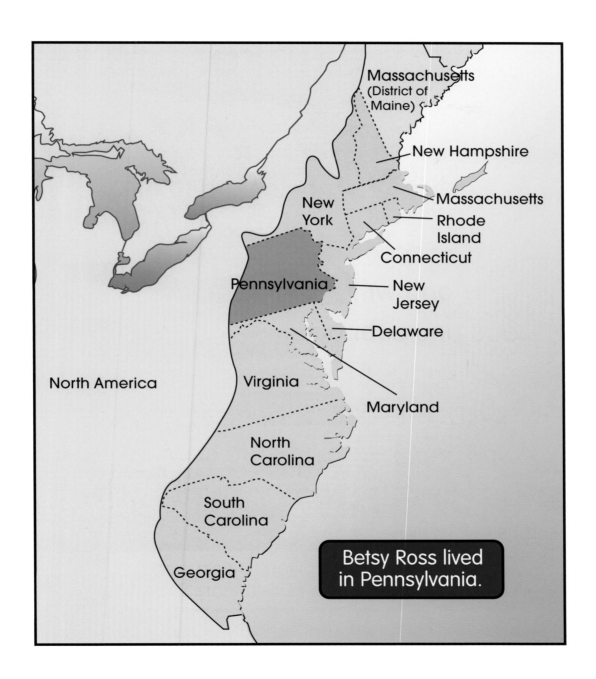

Massachusetts
(District of Maine)

New Hampshire

New York

Massachusetts

Rhode Island

Connecticut

Pennsylvania

New Jersey

Delaware

North America

Virginia

Maryland

North Carolina

South Carolina

Georgia

Betsy Ross lived in Pennsylvania.

Quaker Life

Betsy's family belonged to the Religious Society of Friends. They were Quakers. Quakers believe in God. The Griscoms went to Quaker meetings to worship. They went every week.

The Griscoms lived a simple life. They wore plain clothes. Quakers did not play music, dance, or play cards. They believed in school and hard work.

William Penn was a famous Quaker.

Learning Upholstery

Betsy stopped going to school at age 12. Her father wanted her to learn a trade. So, Betsy became an apprentice at an upholstery shop. She worked for John Webster.

Betsy enjoyed working at Webster's upholstery shop. Back then, an upholstery shop did many things. They sewed fabric on chairs. They made curtains, carpets, blankets, tents, flags, and tablecloths. Upholsterers also hung wallpaper and stuffed mattresses.

Meeting John Ross

Betsy met another apprentice at Webster's upholstery shop. His name was John Ross. They became good friends. One day, Betsy and John decided to get married.

Betsy's parents wanted her to marry a Quaker. John Ross was not a Quaker. He belonged to the Church of England. So, Betsy and John had a secret wedding in New Jersey.

George Fox started the Quaker religion.

Betsy and John Ross were married in November 1773. Betsy stopped going to Quaker meetings. She and her husband joined the Christ Church in Philadelphia, Pennsylvania.

Betsy and John Ross went to the Christ Church in Philadelphia.

American Revolution

Over time, some colonists became unhappy with British laws. They complained about British taxes.

Fights broke out between the British and the unhappy colonists.

Some colonists talked about breaking away from Britain. People who felt this way were called Patriots. Betsy and John were Patriots.

In April 1775, a battle broke out between British troops and colonists. This was the beginning of the Revolutionary War.

Patriot Paul Revere is famous for warning colonists that British troops were near.

In 1775, Betsy and John ran their own upholstery shop. John also worked for Philadelphia's militia. The militia protected Philadelphia in times of need.

One night, John Ross was guarding army supplies. He was hurt in a gunpowder explosion. John Ross died on January 21, 1776.

This upholstery shop is working on a couch.

Legend Of The Flag

Betsy Ross made many flags for the State Navy Board of Pennsylvania. No one is sure if she made the first Stars and Stripes flag. But her story has become an American legend.

The Grand Union flag was common before the Revolutionary War.

George Washington may have asked
Betsy to make a flag with stars and stripes.

According to legend, George Washington visited Betsy in June 1776. He asked her to sew a flag with 13 stripes and 13 stars.

George Washington became the first president of the United States.

America's first national flag had 13 stars and 13 stripes.

Legend says that Betsy advised Washington on the flag. She told him five-sided stars would be best. On June 14, 1777, the Stars and Stripes became America's flag.

Today there are 50 stars on the United States's flag.

Famous Patriot

Betsy Ross married two more times. She had seven daughters in all. Betsy had many grandchildren, too. She enjoyed telling them stories about her life. Betsy Ross died on January 30, 1836.

One of Betsy Ross's grandchildren was William Canby. William wrote a paper about his grandmother in 1870. His paper told Betsy's story about making the first American flag.

Today, Betsy's Philadelphia home is an American landmark. She lived and worked there from 1773 to 1786. Many people believe the first Stars and Stripes was made there, too.

The home of Betsy Ross in Philadelphia, Pennsylvania.

Important Dates

January 1, 1752 Elizabeth "Betsy" Griscom is born.

November 1773 Betsy marries John Ross.

April 1775 The Revolutionary War begins.

January 21, 1776 John Ross dies.

July 4, 1776 American leaders sign the Declaration of Independence.

June 14, 1777 The Stars and Stripes becomes the flag of the United States.

October 19, 1781 America wins the Revolutionary War.

January 30, 1836 Betsy Ross dies.

1870 William Canby says Betsy Ross sewed the first Stars and Stripes flag.

Important Words

apprentice someone who learns a trade from skilled workers.

colony a settlement. Colonists are the people who live in a colony.

landmark an important building.

legend an old story that cannot be proven true.

Patriot the name for colonists who believed in the American Revolution.

Revolutionary War the war Americans fought to win their freedom from Britain.

tax money charged by a city or country.

Web Sites

To learn more about Betsy Ross, visit ABDO Publishing Company on the World Wide Web at www.abdopublishing.com. Web sites about Betsy Ross are featured on our Book Links page. These links are routinely monitored and updated to provide the most current information available.

Index

SEP 1 8

Simple Machines
Inclined Planes

by Martha E. H. Rustad

CAPSTONE PRESS
a capstone imprint

Little Pebble is published by Capstone Press,
1710 Roe Crest Drive, North Mankato, Minnesota 56003
www.mycapstone.com

Library of Congress Cataloging-in-Publication Data
Names: Rustad, Martha E. H. (Martha Elizabeth Hillman), 1975– author.
Title: Inclined planes / by Martha E.H. Rustad.
Description: North Mankato, Minnesota : Capstone Press, 2018. | Series:
    Little pebble. Simple machines
Identifiers: LCCN 2017031581 (print) | LCCN 2017035879 (ebook) |
    ISBN 9781543500899 (eBook PDF) | ISBN 9781543500776 (hardcover) |
    ISBN 9781543500837 (paperback)
Subjects: LCSH: Inclined planes—Juvenile literature.
Classification: LCC TJ147 (ebook) | LCC TJ147 .R877 2018 (print) | DDC
    621.8—dc23
LC record available at https://lccn.loc.gov/2017031581

Editorial Credits

Marissa Kirkman, editor; Kyle Grentz (cover) and Charmaine Whitman (interior), designers;
Jo Miller, media researcher; Katy LaVigne, production specialist

Image Credits

Capstone Studio: Karon Dubke, 17, 21; iStockphoto: /kali9, 11, Shinyfamily, 15; Science
Source: Photo Researchers, Inc., 7; Shutterstock: BCFC, 9, Caron Badkin, 13, Grandpa, 22,
Marcel Derweduwen, cover, 1, Sajee Rod, 5, wavebreakmedia, 19

Design Elements
Capstone

Printed and bound in the USA.
010766S18

Table of Contents

Help with Work

Work is hard!

We need help.

Use a simple machine.

These tools help us work.

inclined plane

An inclined plane is a ramp. We move a load up or down the ramp.

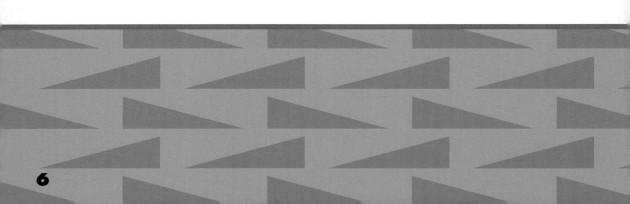

load

ramp

Move a Load

One end is low.

The other end is high.

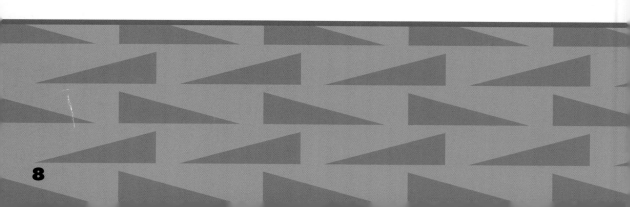

A load sits at the bottom.

We move it up.

load

11

The load moves to the top.

It takes longer to get there.

But the work is easier.

Everyday Tools

The train is at the bottom.

Push!

The train goes up the ramp.

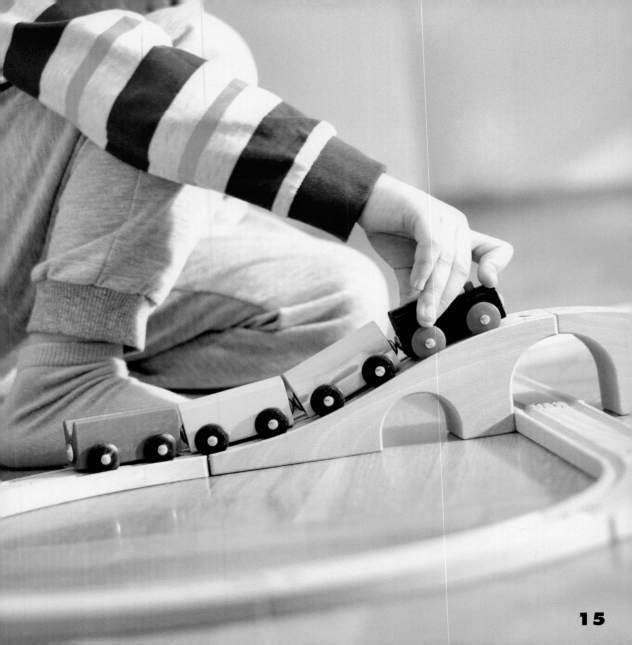

A slide is an inclined plane.

Whee!

I go down fast.

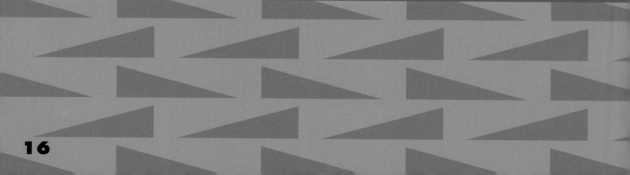

Steps are an inclined plane.

Climb!

We can reach the top.

We use a simple machine.

It makes work easier and fun.

Glossary

inclined plane—a simple machine that makes moving a load up or down easier; it is sloped with one end higher than the other, like a ramp

load—an object that you want to move or lift

simple machine—a tool that makes it easier to do something

tool—an item used to make work easier

work—a job that must be done

Read More

Miller, Tim and Rebecca Sjonger. *Inclined Planes in My Makerspace.* Simple Machines in My Makerspace. New York: Crabtree Publishing, 2017.

Schuh, Mari. *Playing a Game: Inclined Plane vs. Lever.* Simple Machines to the Rescue. Minneapolis: Lerner, 2016.

Weakland, Mark. *Fred Flintstone's Adventures with Inclined Planes: A Rampin' Good Time.* Flintstones Explain Simple Machines. North Mankato, Minn.: Capstone Press, 2016.

Internet Sites

Use FactHound to find Internet sites related to this book.

Visit www.facthound.com

Just type in 9781543500776 and go.

 Super-cool stuff! Check out projects, games and lots more at **www.capstonekids.com**

Critical Thinking Questions

1. What do we move up or down a ramp?

2. What is different about the two ends of an inclined plane?

3. What types of inclined planes have you used? How did they help you?

Index